# Comprehensive Aphasia Test

Kate Swinburn, Gillian Porter and David Howard

SCRIPT and
SCORING BOOKLET

CLIENT'S NAME: _____    DATE OF BIRTH: _____

ADMINISTRATOR'S NAME: _____    DATE: _____

# Comprehensive Aphasia Test: Script and Scoring Booklet

## (master score sheet at end of booklet)

Please read the Manual before administering the CAT and use the Manual in conjunction with this Scoring Booklet for both assessment and scoring.

**Read aloud the text that is italicised**. Follow all other instructions.

## THE COGNITIVE SCREEN

## 1. LINE BISECTION

**GIVE THIS SCORING BOOK** to the **person with aphasia** and turn to the next page (p. 2); rotate the book so that the lines are horizontal.

*I want you to cut these lines in half like this, do you see the line is in two halves now? You try with this line.*

Give AS MANY DEMONSTRATION items as you feel are necessary to establish comprehension of the task. Indicate to the person that you want him/her to do the same with the three lines on p. 5 WITHOUT POINTING directly to each test line (ensure they use a black or blue pen).

*Here's your page. Can you cut all these lines in half?*

Use the Line Bisection Scores Template on p. 5 (which could be photocopied onto an acetate for easier use) to determine scores.

Score line 1     . . . . . . . . . . . . . . . . . . . . . . .

Score line 2     . . . . . . . . . . . . . . . . . . . . . . .

Score line 3     . . . . . . . . . . . . . . . . . . . . . . .

TOTAL     . . . . . . . . . . . . . . . . . . . . . . .

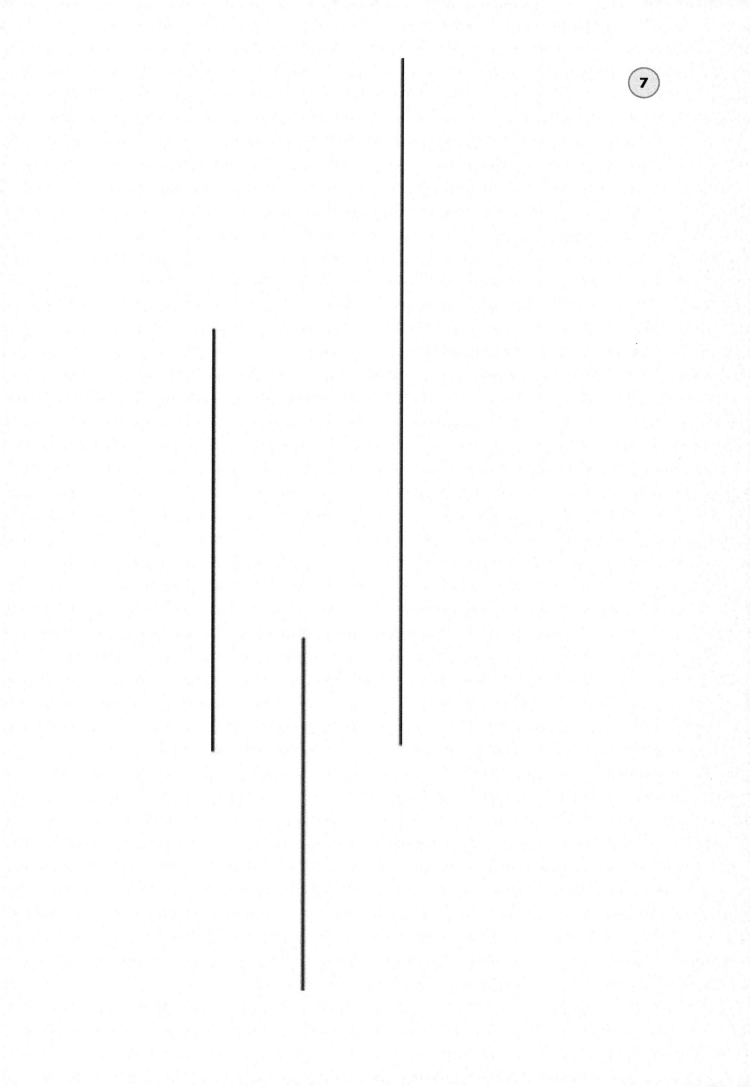

## 2.   SEMANTIC MEMORY (PP. 1–11 C&L)

*You see we have a picture here* [point to the monkey on p. 1 of the Cognitive & Language Test Book (C&L)] *– and one in each corner* [point to four picture choices]. *Which of these corner pictures goes best with this middle picture – which one is MOST ASSOCIATED?* (Gesture to aid comprehension.)

   Show the practice item. This practice item can be done as often as needed. Proceed with the test items (give encouragement but not feedback).

| | TARGET | | CLOSE SEMANTIC DISTRACTOR | | DISTANT SEMANTIC DISTRACTOR | | UNRELATED DISTRACTOR | |
|---|---|---|---|---|---|---|---|---|
| P | banana | ✓ | pear | | chocolate | | envelope | |
| 1 | eye | | ear | | mouth | | elephant | |
| 2 | mitten | | sock | | jersey | | lighthouse | |
| 3 | candle | | light bulb | | radio | | star | |
| 4 | bed | | chair | | stool | | flag | |
| 5 | igloo | | hut | | house | | sunshade | |
| 6 | arm | | leg | | neck | | tortoise | |
| 7 | church | | school | | factory | | skate | |
| 8 | fire | | torch | | rocket | | picture | |
| 9 | clown | | ballerina | | priest | | sheep | |
| 10 | watering can | | bucket | | shower | | anchor | |
| **Total** | | **/10** | | **/10** | | **/10** | | **/10** |

Leave a gap of approximately **three minutes** between the end of the "Semantic memory" and the beginning of the "Recognition memory" subtests. During this time, complete the "Word fluency" subtest.

## 3. WORD FLUENCY (PP. 13–16 C&L)

*I'm going to give you a minute.*
*Say out loud all the words that go in a category.*
*I'll give you an example . . . if I gave you the category "clothes"* [point to written word on p. 13]
*you might say . . . trousers, shirt, jumper, etc. . . . but your category isn't clothes, it's animals . . .*
*you've got to say as many animals as you can in a minute.* (Repeat procedure for "s" words.)

For the practice item, show the word "clothes" and say some examples to demonstrate task requirements. Then show the written word "animals" in the C&L Test Book, say the word, and ask the person to name as many animals as possible. Write down responses in 15-second groupings. Then do the same with the letters. Demonstrate with the letter "b", and then ask the person to produce as many words as they can beginning with the letter "s" (p. 16). (If the person with aphasia supplies a proper noun, say "No names, please".)

| TIME BAND | ANIMALS | "S" |
|---|---|---|
| 0–15 seconds | | |
| 15–30 seconds | | |
| 30–45 seconds | | |
| 45–60 seconds | | |
| No. of items named | | |

# 4.   RECOGNITION MEMORY (PP. 18–28 C&L)

*One of these pictures you've seen before in this test* [flick through previous pages without showing any of them specifically]. *Which one did you see before?*

| P | TARGET | | TOP LEFT | TOP RIGHT | BOTTOM LEFT | BOTTOM RIGHT |
|---|--------|---|----------|-----------|-------------|--------------|
| P | *monkey* | | *scissors* | *foot* | *teapot* | ***monkey*** |
| 1 | glasses | | shoe | **glasses** | table | piano |
| 2 | hand | | soldier | frog | **hand** | axe |
| 3 | matches | | nest | **matches** | bicycle | saw |
| 4 | pillow | | pineapple | seahorse | **pillow** | kayak |
| 5 | Eskimo | | racquet | basket | television | **Eskimo** |
| 6 | watch | | tulip | **watch** | cot | wool |
| 7 | nun | | **nun** | fish | tree | telephone |
| 8 | tent | | **tent** | kite | castle | lifebelt |
| 9 | mask | | nose | barber | **mask** | sailor |
| 10 | flower | | cat | camel | fir tree | **flower** |
| | **TOTAL** | | **/10** | | | |

## 5.  GESTURE OBJECT USE (PP. 30–36 C&L)

*I want you to imagine I've put this object in your hand* [gesture]. *SHOW ME what you do with it.*

Keep Test Book out of reach to encourage gesturing rather than pointing.

| | TARGET | SCORE | | | MANNER OF RESPONSE* | | | COMMENT |
|---|---|---|---|---|---|---|---|---|
| P | pen | 0 | 1 | 2 | A | O | BPO | |
| 1 | peg | 0 | 1 | 2 | A | O | BPO | |
| 2 | comb | 0 | 1 | 2 | A | O | BPO | |
| 3 | mug | 0 | 1 | 2 | A | O | BPO | |
| 4 | scissors | 0 | 1 | 2 | A | O | BPO | |
| 5 | toothbrush | 0 | 1 | 2 | A | O | BPO | |
| 6 | paintbrush | 0 | 1 | 2 | A | O | BPO | |
| | **TOTAL** | **/12** | | | | | | |

* 2 = Gesture correct with no ambiguity
  1 = Action (A) or orientation (O) is incorrect, or if body part is used as object (BPO)
  0 = Incorrect

## 6.  ARITHMETIC

*Can you show me the answer to these sums please?*
Go to next page (with arithmetic items).
Do **NOT** indicate the change of calculation type (e.g., addition/subtraction).
Ask the person to write in the correct answer or point to the correct answer to each sum (multiple choice). Underline the response.

Total =  /6

# [THIS IS THE END OF THE COGNITIVE SECTION]

$9 + 6 =$      (8     13     15     19     21)

$7 - 4 =$      (2     3     4     11     6)

$8 \times 7 =$      (15     42     54     56     76)

$14 + 18 =$      (21     22     28     32     3)

$34 - 15 =$      (11     19     21     29     4)

$147 + 58 =$      (89     91     99     101     205)

Scoring system:

0 = incorrect

1 = correct after repetition of stimulus (R), self-correction (Sc) or significant delay (over 5 seconds) (D)

2 = correct with no assistance or delay

---

## PART 1: LANGUAGE COMPREHENSION

### 7.    COMPREHENSION OF SPOKEN WORDS (PP. 38–53 C&L)

*I'm going to say a word.*

*I want you to point to the picture that goes best with that word.*

*Can you find me "mouse"? That's fine . . . there is always a picture that is close but not quite right* [point to "mouse" and "rabbit"] *. . . it's there to catch you out, so be careful.*

TIME for 5 seconds. DISCONTINUE if the person makes four consecutive failures.

| | TARGET | MANNER OF RESPONSE | | | SCORE | | | PHONOLOGICAL DISTRACTOR | NO. OF FEATURES DIFFERENT & POSITION | | SEMANTIC DISTRACTOR | UNRELATED DISTRACTOR |
|---|---|---|---|---|---|---|---|---|---|---|---|---|
| P | *mouse* | | | | | | | *house* | *3df* | *I* | *rabbit* | *church* |
| 1 | ship | D | Sc | R | 0 | 1 | 2 | lip | 2df | I | boat | nose |
| 2 | goat | D | Sc | R | 0 | 1 | 2 | coat | 1df | I | sheep | dress |
| 3 | horn | D | Sc | R | 0 | 1 | 2 | horse | 2df | F | trumpet | cow |
| 4 | boat | D | Sc | R | 0 | 1 | 2 | bone | 2df | F | canoe | heart |
| 5 | dart | D | Sc | R | 0 | 1 | 2 | cart | 2df | I | arrow | horse |
| 6 | knee | D | Sc | R | 0 | 1 | 2 | bee | 2df | I | elbow | spider |
| 7 | pear | D | Sc | R | 0 | 1 | 2 | bear | 1df | I | apple | lion |
| 8 | tyre | D | Sc | R | 0 | 1 | 2 | fire | 2df | I | wheel | matches |
| 9 | leek | D | Sc | R | 0 | 1 | 2 | leaf | 2df | F | carrot | flowers |
| 10 | kettle | D | Sc | R | 0 | 1 | 2 | kennel | 2df | M | teapot | cage |
| 11 | hen | D | Sc | R | 0 | 1 | 2 | head | 1df | F | cockerel | foot |
| 12 | roof | D | Sc | R | 0 | 1 | 2 | hoof | 2df | I | chimney | tail |
| 13 | pine | D | Sc | R | 0 | 1 | 2 | pipe | 3df | F | palm tree | cigarette |
| 14 | bull | D | Sc | R | 0 | 1 | 2 | wool | 1df | I | cow | cotton |
| 15 | door | D | Sc | R | 0 | 1 | 2 | saw | 2df | I | window | hammer |
| | | | | | ( /15) | /30 | | /15 | | | /15 | /15 |

# 8. COMPREHENSION OF WRITTEN WORDS (PP. 55–70 C&L)

*This is the same idea, only this time the word is written down for you there, I don't say anything.*
*So which picture goes with that word [point to the word "rocket"]?*

TIME for 5 seconds. DISCONTINUE if the person makes four consecutive failures.

| | TARGET | MANNER OF RESPONSE | | SCORE | | | PHONOLOGICAL DISTRACTOR | NO. OF FEATURES DIFFERENT & POSITION | | SEMANTIC DISTRACTOR | UNRELATED DISTRACTOR |
|---|---|---|---|---|---|---|---|---|---|---|---|
| P | rocket | | | | | | pocket | 3df | I | aeroplane | sleeve |
| 1 | mug | D | Sc | 0 | 1 | 2 | rug | 2df | I | cup | carpet |
| 2 | pin | D | Sc | 0 | 1 | 2 | bin | 1df | I | needle | basket |
| 3 | cap | D | Sc | 0 | 1 | 2 | cat | 1df | F | hat | dog |
| 4 | nail | D | Sc | 0 | 1 | 2 | tail | 2df | I | screw | leg |
| 5 | wall | D | Sc | 0 | 1 | 2 | ball | 1df | I | fence | toys |
| 6 | boots | D | Sc | 0 | 1 | 2 | roots | 2df | I | shoes | branches |
| 7 | pen | D | Sc | 0 | 1 | 2 | peg | 2df | F | pencil | safety pin |
| 8 | rose | D | Sc | 0 | 1 | 2 | rope | 3df | F | tulip | chain |
| 9 | bag | D | Sc | 0 | 1 | 2 | bat | 2df | F | case | owl |
| 10 | boy | D | Sc | 0 | 1 | 2 | toy | 2df | I | girl | dice |
| 11 | pig | D | Sc | 0 | 1 | 2 | wig | 2df | I | cow | hat |
| 12 | lock | D | Sc | 0 | 1 | 2 | log | 1df | I | key | tree |
| 13 | sun | D | Sc | 0 | 1 | 2 | nun | 2df | I | moon | mayor |
| 14 | book | D | Sc | 0 | 1 | 2 | hook | 3df | I | newspaper | noose |
| 15 | grass | D | Sc | 0 | 1 | 2 | glass | 1df | M | flowers | bottle |
| | | | | ( /15) /30 | | | /15 | | | /15 | /15 |

# 9. COMPREHENSION OF SPOKEN SENTENCES (PP. 72–88 C&L)

*This is similar – only this time I say a **sentence** not a word. So you have to point to the picture that goes best with this sentence . . . ready?*

TIME for 5 seconds from the moment of saying the target sentence.
DISCONTINUE if the person makes four consecutive failures.

| | SENTENCE TYPE† | TARGET SENTENCE | SELECTION | RESPONSE | SCORE |
|---|---|---|---|---|---|
| P | NP VP (1) | **A The woman is sitting**<br>B The woman is *standing*<br>C The *man* is *standing*<br>D The *man* is sitting | **A** B C D | D Sc R | 0 1 2 |
| 1 | NP VP (1) | **B The woman is drinking**<br>A The woman is *eating*<br>C The *man* is drinking<br>D The *man* is *eating* | A **B** C D | D Sc R | 0 1 2 |
| 2 | NP VP (1) | **C The man is walking**<br>A The *woman* is *standing*<br>B The *woman* is walking<br>D The man is *standing* | A B **C** D | D Sc R | 0 1 2 |
| 3 | NP VP (1) | **C She is laughing**<br>A *He* is laughing<br>B She is *crying*<br>D *He* is *crying* | A B **C** D | D Sc R | 0 1 2 |
| 4 | NP VP NP (2) I/A | **D The man is eating the apple**<br>A The *woman* is eating the apple<br>B The *woman* is eating an *ice-cream*<br>C The man is eating an *ice-cream* | A B C **D** | D Sc R | 0 1 2 |
| 5 | NP VP NP (2) I/A | **B The woman is painting a wall**<br>A The woman is painting a *picture*<br>C The *man* is painting a *picture*<br>D The *man* is painting a wall | A **B** C D | D Sc R | 0 1 2 |
| 6 | NP VP PP (2) I | **A The dog is sitting on the table**<br>B The dog is sitting *under* the table<br>C The *boy* is sitting on the table<br>D The *boy* is sitting *under* the table | **A** B C D | D Sc R | 0 1 2 |
| 7 | NP VP NP (2) R | **B The apple is under the shoe**<br>A The *pen* is under the *paper*<br>C The *shoe* is under the *apple*<br>D The *paper* is under the *pen* | A **B** C D | D Sc R | 0 1 2 |

| | SENTENCE TYPE† | TARGET SENTENCE | SELECTION | RESPONSE | SCORE |
|---|---|---|---|---|---|
| 8 | NP VP NP (2) R/A | **B The nurse shoots the butcher**<br>A The *butcher* shoots the *nurse*<br>C The *butcher chases* the *nurse*<br>D The nurse *chases* the butcher | A **B** C D | D Sc R | 0 1 2 |
| 9 | NP VP NP (2) R/A | **C The singer hits the soldier**<br>A The singer *photographs* the soldier<br>B The *soldier photographs* the *singer*<br>D The *soldier* hits the *singer* | A B **C** D | D Sc R | 0 1 2 |
| 10 | NP VP PP (2) R/P | **A The policeman is painted by the dancer**<br>B The *dancer* is *chased* by the *policeman*<br>C The *dancer* is painted by the *policeman*<br>D The policeman is *chased* by the dancer | **A** B C D | D Sc R | 0 1 2 |
| 11 | NP VP PP (2) R/P | **D The butcher is chased by the nurse**<br>A The *nurse* is *killed* by the *butcher*<br>B The butcher is *killed* by the nurse<br>C The *nurse* is chased by the *butcher* | A B C **D** | D Sc R | 0 1 2 |
| 12 | NP VP NP (2) R/A | **A The dancer paints the policeman**<br>B The *policeman chases* the *dancer*<br>C The *policeman* paints the *dancer*<br>D The dancer *chases* the policeman | **A** B C D | D Sc R | 0 1 2 |
| 13 | NP (*PP) VP NP (2) R/E | **D The shoe under the pencil is blue**<br>A (*shoe-under-pencil-blue*)**<br>B The shoe *on* the pencil is blue<br>C The *pencil* under the *shoe* is blue | A B C **D** | D Sc R | 0 1 2 |
| 14 | NP (*clause) VP NP (2) E | **A The carpet the cat is on is red**<br>B The *red cat* is on the carpet<br>C/D Irrelevant | **A** B C D | D Sc R | 0 1 2 |
| 15 | NP VP PP (2) R | **C The red pencil is under the shoe**<br>A The red pencil is *on* the shoe<br>B The *green* pencil is under the shoe<br>D The red *shoe* is under the *pencil* | A B **C** D | D Sc R | 0 1 2 |
| 16 | NP (*PP) VP NP | **D The flower in the cup is blue**<br>A The flower *under* the cup is blue<br>B The flower *under* the cup is *green*<br>C (*flower-in-cup-blue*)** | A B C **D** | D Sc R | 0 1 2 |
| | **TOTAL** | | | ( /16) | /32 |

†Key: A = active sentence; P = passive sentence; R = reversible sentence; I = irreversible sentence; E = embedded sentence; ( ) = number of predicates; * = post-modifying; ** = using word order alone to comprehend this sentence

## 10.  COMPREHENSION OF WRITTEN SENTENCES
## (PP. 90–106 C&L)

*This time the sentences are written for you here – I don't say anything. When you're ready, point to the picture that goes with that sentence* [point to the written sentence].

TIME for 5 seconds from when you've read the sentence to yourself.

DISCONTINUE if the person makes four consecutive failures.

| | SENTENCE TYPE† | TARGET SENTENCE | SELECTION | RESPONSE | SCORE |
|---|---|---|---|---|---|
| P | NP VP (1) | **D The man is sitting**<br>A The *woman* is sitting<br>B The *woman* is *standing*<br>C The man is *standing* | A  B  C  **D** | D          Sc | 0   1   2 |
| 1 | NP VP (1) | **C The man is drinking**<br>A The *woman* is *eating*<br>B The *woman* is drinking<br>D The man is *eating* | A  B  **C**  D | D          Sc | 0   1   2 |
| 2 | NP VP (1) | **B The woman is walking**<br>A The woman is *standing*<br>C The *man* is walking<br>D The *man* is *standing* | A  **B**  C  D | D          Sc | 0   1   2 |
| 3 | NP VP (1) | **D He is crying**<br>A He is *laughing*<br>B *She* is crying<br>C *She* is *laughing* | A  B  C  **D** | D          Sc | 0   1   2 |
| 4 | NP VP NP (2) I/A | **B The woman is eating an ice-cream**<br>A The woman is eating an *apple*<br>C The *man* is eating an ice-cream<br>D The *man* is eating an *apple* | A  **B**  C  D | D          Sc | 0   1   2 |
| 5 | NP VP NP (2) I/A | **C The man is painting a picture**<br>A The *woman* is painting a picture<br>B The *woman* is painting a *wall*<br>D The man is painting a *wall* | A  B  **C**  D | D          Sc | 0   1   2 |
| 6 | NP VP PP (2) I | **D The boy is sitting under the table**<br>A The *dog* is sitting *on* the table<br>B The *dog* is sitting under the table<br>C The boy is sitting *on* the table | A  B  C  **D** | D          Sc | 0   1   2 |
| 7 | NP VP NP (2) R | **A The pen is under the paper**<br>B The *apple* is under the *shoe*<br>C The *shoe* is under the *apple*<br>D The *paper* is under the *pen* | **A**  B  C  D | D          Sc | 0   1   2 |

| | SENTENCE TYPE[†] | TARGET SENTENCE | SELECTION | RESPONSE | SCORE |
|---|---|---|---|---|---|
| 8 | NP VP NP<br><br>(2)<br><br>R/A | **A The butcher shoots the nurse**<br>B The *nurse* shoots the *butcher*<br>C The butcher *chases* the nurse<br>D The *nurse chases* the *butcher* | **A** B C D | D    Sc | 0   1   2 |
| 9 | NP VP NP<br><br>(2)<br><br>R/A | **D The soldier hits the singer**<br>A The *singer photographs* the *soldier*<br>B The soldier *photographs* the singer<br>C The *singer* hits the *soldier* | A B C **D** | D    Sc | 0   1   2 |
| 10 | NP VP PP<br><br>(2)<br><br>R/P | **C The dancer is painted by the policeman**<br>A The *policeman* is painted by the *dancer*<br>B The dancer is *chased* by the policeman<br>D The *policeman* is *chased* by the *dancer* | A B **C** D | D    Sc | 0   1   2 |
| 11 | NP VP PP<br><br>(2)<br><br>R/P | **C The nurse is chased by the butcher**<br>A The nurse is *killed* by the butcher<br>B The *butcher* is *killed* by the *nurse*<br>D The *butcher* is chased by the *nurse* | A B **C** D | D    Sc | 0   1   2 |
| 12 | NP VP NP<br><br>(2)<br><br>R/A | **C The policeman paints the dancer**<br>A The *dancer* paints the *policeman*<br>B The policeman *chases* the dancer<br>D The *dancer chases* the *policeman* | A B **C** D | D    Sc | 0   1   2 |
| 13 | NP (*PP)<br>VP NP<br>(2)<br>R/E | **D The shoe under the pencil is red**<br>A (*shoe-under-pencil-red*)**<br>B The *pencil* under the *shoe* is red<br>C The shoe *on* the pencil is red | A B C **D** | D    Sc | 0   1   2 |
| 14 | NP (*clause)<br>VP NP<br>(2)<br>R/E | **B The carpet the cat is on is green**<br>C The *green cat* is on the carpet<br>A/D Irrelevant | A **B** C D | D    Sc | 0   1   2 |
| 15 | NP VP PP<br><br>(2)<br><br>R | **A The blue shoe is under the pencil**<br>B The blue *pencil* is under the *shoe*<br>C The blue shoe is *on* the pencil<br>D The *red* shoe is under the pencil | **A** B C D | D    Sc | 0   1   2 |
| 16 | NP (*PP)<br>VP NP<br>R | **B The flower under the cup is red**<br>A (*flower-under-cup-red*)**<br>C The flower *in* the cup is red<br>D The *cup* under the *flower* is red | A **B** C D | D    Sc | 0   1   2 |
| | **TOTAL** | | | | **/32** |

[†]Key: A = active sentence; P = passive sentence; R = reversible sentence; I = irreversible sentence; E = embedded sentence; ( ) = number of predicates; * = post-modifying; ** = using word order alone to comprehend this sentence

## 11. COMPREHENSION OF SPOKEN PARAGRAPHS (P. 108 C&L)

*I'm going to read you a short story. I want you to listen and then answer some questions. You should only say yes or no [point to yes/no on p. 108 C&L]. Are you ready?*

*Sally and Richard had been on the train for over three hours. They were tired and fed up. The train was already 45 minutes late, the buffet had closed so there was no food, and the lady opposite was snoring.*

| | | |
|---|---|---|
| a. | Were Sally and Richard travelling by car? | Yes/**No** |
| b. | Were they on time? | Yes/**No** |
| a. | Were they travelling by train? | **Yes**/No |
| b. | Were they early? | Yes/**No**    /2 |

*OK – here's another one. Are you ready?*

*The explosion in central London caused havoc. Initially terrorists were suspected but it turned out not to be a bomb. The cause was found to be a burst gas main that ignited when someone had thrown down a lighted cigarette. People three miles away heard the explosion and the damage is estimated at over a million pounds.*

| | | |
|---|---|---|
| a. | Was the explosion in Leicester? | Yes/**No** |
| b. | Was it caused by a bomb? | Yes/**No** |
| a. | Was it in London? | **Yes**/No |
| b. | Was the explosion caused by a gas main? | **Yes**/No    /2 |

TOTAL CORRECT          /4

# [THIS IS THE END OF THE LANGUAGE COMPREHENSION SECTION]

# PART 2: EXPRESSIVE LANGUAGE

## 12. REPETITION OF WORDS

*I'm going to say some words and I'd like you just to repeat them back to me.*
  *Ready?* (Read the target words from the table below.)

|   | TARGET | IMAG | | FREQ | | LENGTH (SYLLABLES) | | RESPONSE | MANNER OF RESPONSE | SCORE |
|---|--------|------|---|------|---|---|---|----------|--------------------|-------|
| P | *table* | | | | | | | | | |
| 1 | vine | H | | | | L | 1 | | D  Sc  R | 0  1  2 |
| 2 | president | H | | H | | | 3 | | D  Sc  R | 0  1  2 |
| 3 | scorn | | L | | | L | 1 | | D  Sc  R | 0  1  2 |
| 4 | radio | H | | H | | | 3 | | D  Sc  R | 0  1  2 |
| 5 | crucifix | H | | | | L | 3 | | D  Sc  R | 0  1  2 |
| 6 | trade | | L | H | | | 1 | | D  Sc  R | 0  1  2 |
| 7 | etiquette | | L | | | L | 3 | | D  Sc  R | 0  1  2 |
| 8 | plant | H | | H | | | 1 | | D  Sc  R | 0  1  2 |
| 9 | tomato | H | | | | L | 3 | | D  Sc  R | 0  1  2 |
| 10 | character | | L | H | | | 3 | | D  Sc  R | 0  1  2 |
| 11 | gilt | | L | | | L | 1 | | D  Sc  R | 0  1  2 |
| 12 | gravity | | L | | | L | 3 | | D  Sc  R | 0  1  2 |
| 13 | swamp | H | | | | L | 1 | | D  Sc  R | 0  1  2 |
| 14 | evidence | | L | H | | | 3 | | D  Sc  R | 0  1  2 |
| 15 | face | H | | H | | | 1 | | D  Sc  R | 0  1  2 |
| 16 | mind | | L | H | | | 1 | | D  Sc  R | 0  1  2 |
| | | /8 | /8 | /8 | /8 | /8 | /8 | | **TOTAL ( /16)** | **/32** |

Key: IMAG = imageability; FREQ = frequency; H = high; L = low

## 13. REPETITION OF COMPLEX WORDS

Continue reading the target words from the table below.

|   | TARGET | RESPONSE | MANNER OF RESPONSE | SCORE |
|---|--------|----------|--------------------|-------|
| 1 | unthinkable | | D  Sc  R | 0  1  2 |
| 2 | defrosted | | D  Sc  R | 0  1  2 |
| 3 | conforming | | D  Sc  R | 0  1  2 |
| | | | **TOTAL ( /3)** | **/6** |

## 14. REPETITION OF NONWORDS

*Now there are some nonsense words, made-up words. If you find yourself saying a real word you've got it wrong. **All** these words are nonsense.*

Read the target words from the table below.

| | TARGET | RESPONSE | MANNER OF RESPONSE | | | SCORE | | |
|---|---|---|---|---|---|---|---|---|
| 1 | gart | | D | Sc | R | 0 | 1 | 2 |
| 2 | clup | | D | Sc | R | 0 | 1 | 2 |
| 3 | spenk | | D | Sc | R | 0 | 1 | 2 |
| 4 | trimpy | | D | Sc | R | 0 | 1 | 2 |
| 5 | prastode | | D | Sc | R | 0 | 1 | 2 |
| | | | **TOTAL (  /5)** | | | | | **/10** |

## 15. REPETITION OF DIGIT STRINGS

*Now I'm going to say a string of numbers starting with two numbers and working up. So can you repeat these number strings? Ready?*

Read out the FIRST LINE of each level. If the response is CORRECT, move on to the first line of the next level. If the response is INCORRECT, read out the second line of that level.

| LEVEL | STIMULUS | RESPONSE (phonemic/dyspraxic errors ARE accepted) |
|---|---|---|
| 2 items | 7  2<br>1  3 | |
| 3 items | 6  3  5<br>2  9  8 | |
| 4 items | 4  5  2  7<br>5  6  9  1 | |
| 5 items | 6  2  9  7  5<br>7  6  8  1  3 | |
| 6 items | 7  8  4  1  6  9<br>3  6  8  2  9  4 | |
| 7 items | 2  8  7  4  5  1  2<br>7  2  8  6  4  5  3 | |
| | To obtain score, double the maximum length repeated correctly | (DIGIT SPAN    2    3    4    5    6    7)<br>**TOTAL SCORE**                                    **/14** |

# 16. REPETITION OF SENTENCES

*Now I'm going to say a sentence. Can you repeat each word that I've said? Ready?*

Read out the FIRST SENTENCE of each level. If the person with aphasia repeats it CORRECTLY, move to the next level. If he/she FAILS, asks him/her to repeat the SECOND SENTENCE of that level. Write the response verbatim here.

| No. CONTENT WORDS | | STIMULUS (phonemic and obviously dyspraxic errors ARE accepted) |
|---|---|---|
| 3 (5) | | The **cat chased** the **bird** |
| | Response: | |
| | | The **girl eats** the **apple** |
| | Response: | |
| 4 (7) | | The **man went** and **shut** the **window** |
| | Response: | |
| | | They **decided** to **paint** the **room blue** |
| | Response: | |
| 5 (9) | | The **children listened** as the **teacher read** the **story** |
| | Response: | |
| | | The **local map** was **small** and **difficult** to **read** |
| | Response: | |
| 6 (11) | | The **boy** and **girl climbed** the **hill** and **admired** the **view** |
| | Response: | |
| | | It was a **long time before** the **area** was **pronounced safe** |
| | Response: | |
| | | (SENTENCE SPAN    3    4    5    6) To obtain score, double the maximum length repeated correctly  **TOTAL SCORE**    **/12** |

(Number in brackets refers to total number of words)

# 17.  NAMING OBJECTS (PP. 110–134 C&L)

*What's that a picture of?*

If the person with aphasia is unable to name a picture, or names it incorrectly, provide a PHONEMIC CUE. If visual misperception of the picture is suspected, provide a SEMANTIC CUE. DISCONTINUE if there are eight consecutive failures.

See Manual for scoring details.

| | TARGET | FREQ | | IMAG | | LENGTH (SYLLABLES) | | RESPONSE (TRANSCRIPTION) | MANNER OF RESPONSE | | SCORE | | |
|---|---|---|---|---|---|---|---|---|---|---|---|---|---|
| P | car | H | | H | | 1 | | | | | | | |
| 1 | knife | H | | H | | 1 | | | D | Sc | 0 | 1 | 2 |
| 2 | star | H | | H | | 1 | | | D | Sc | 0 | 1 | 2 |
| 3 | spoon | | LIn | | L | 1 | | | D | Sc | 0 | 1 | 2 |
| 4 | cigarette | H | | H | | | 3 | | D | Sc | 0 | 1 | 2 |
| 5 | fox | | LAn | H | | 1 | | | D | Sc | 0 | 1 | 2 |
| 6 | aerial | | LIn | | L | | 3 | | D | Sc | 0 | 1 | 2 |
| 7 | pyramid | | LIn | H | | | 3 | | D | Sc | 0 | 1 | 2 |
| 8 | saxophone | | LIn | H | | | 3 | | D | Sc | 0 | 1 | 2 |
| 9 | pineapple | | LAn | | L | | 3 | | D | Sc | 0 | 1 | 2 |
| 10 | brush | H | | | L | 1 | | | D | Sc | 0 | 1 | 2 |
| 11 | telephone | H | | H | | | 3 | | D | Sc | 0 | 1 | 2 |
| 12 | crab | | LAn | | L | 1 | | | D | Sc | 0 | 1 | 2 |
| 13 | elephant | | LAn | H | | | 3 | | D | Sc | 0 | 1 | 2 |
| 14 | camera | H | | | L | | 3 | | D | Sc | 0 | 1 | 2 |
| 15 | frog | | LAn | H | | 1 | | | D | Sc | 0 | 1 | 2 |
| 16 | snail | | LAn | | L | 1 | | | D | Sc | 0 | 1 | 2 |
| 17 | caravan | | LIn | | L | | 3 | | D | Sc | 0 | 1 | 2 |
| 18 | drum | | LIn | H | | 1 | | | D | Sc | 0 | 1 | 2 |
| 19 | gate | H | | | L | 1 | | | D | Sc | 0 | 1 | 2 |
| 20 | crocodile | | LAn | | L | | 3 | | D | Sc | 0 | 1 | 2 |
| 21 | ski | | LIn | H | | 1 | | | D | Sc | 0 | 1 | 2 |
| 22 | butterfly | | LAn | H | | | 3 | | D | Sc | 0 | 1 | 2 |
| 23 | sock | | LIn | | L | 1 | | | D | Sc | 0 | 1 | 2 |
| 24 | envelope | H | | | L | | 3 | | D | Sc | 0 | 1 | 2 |
| | | /8 | /16 | /12 | /12 | /12 | /12 | **TOTAL SCORE** | ( | /24) | | | /48 |

Key: IMAG = imageability; FREQ = frequency; H = high; L = low; An = animate; In = inanimate

# 18. NAMING ACTIONS (PP. 136–141 C&L)

[Point to the picture of a man eating.] *What's that person **doing?***

    TIME each response and transcribe each one in full.

| | TARGET | RESPONSE (TRANSCRIPTION) | MANNER OF RESPONSE | | SCORE | | |
|---|---|---|---|---|---|---|---|
| P | eating | | | | | | |
| 1 | winding | | D | Sc | 0 | 1 | 2 |
| 2 | sawing | | D | Sc | 0 | 1 | 2 |
| 3 | threading | | D | Sc | 0 | 1 | 2 |
| 4 | typing | | D | Sc | 0 | 1 | 2 |
| 5 | licking | | D | Sc | 0 | 1 | 2 |
| | | **TOTAL SCORE** | ( | /5) | | /10 | |

## 19.    SPOKEN PICTURE DESCRIPTION (P. 143 C&L)

*Tell me what's happening in this picture.*

If the person misses out areas of the picture, point to them and ask "what about that?" or some such prompt.

TRANSCRIBE their response in the space below.

See Manual for scoring, and Appendix 1 for worked examples.

| A<br>APPROPRIATE ICWS | B<br>INAPPROPRIATE ICWS | C<br>SYNTACTIC VARIETY | D<br>GRAMMATICAL<br>WELL-FORMEDNESS | E<br>SPEED |
|---|---|---|---|---|
| | | | | |
| **A Total =** | **B Total =** | **C Total =** | **D Total =** | **E Total =** |

Key: ICWS = information-carrying words

**TOTAL SCORE (A − B) + C + D + E =**

## 20.    READING WORDS (P. 145 C&L)

*Here are some words. Could you read them out aloud for me?*

Cover the preceding words with card if helpful.

| | TARGET | FREQ | | IMAG | | REG | SYLL | RESPONSE | MANNER OF RESPONSE | | SCORE | | |
|---|---|---|---|---|---|---|---|---|---|---|---|---|---|
| P | *chair* | | | | | | | | | | | | |
| 1 | worm | | L | H | | | I | | D | Sc | 0 | 1 | 2 |
| 2 | fraud | | L | | L | R | | | D | Sc | 0 | 1 | 2 |
| 3 | yacht | | L | H | | | I | | D | Sc | 0 | 1 | 2 |
| 4 | hand | H | | H | | R | | | D | Sc | 0 | 1 | 2 |
| 5 | dynasty | | L | | L | | 3 | | D | Sc | 0 | 1 | 2 |
| 6 | horse | H | | H | | R | | | D | Sc | 0 | 1 | 2 |
| 7 | tomato | | L | H | | | 3 | | D | Sc | 0 | 1 | 2 |
| 8 | trout | | L | H | | R | | | D | Sc | 0 | 1 | 2 |
| 9 | break | H | | | L | | I | | D | Sc | 0 | 1 | 2 |
| 10 | vest | | L | H | | R | | | D | Sc | 0 | 1 | 2 |
| 11 | cause | H | | | L | R | | | D | Sc | 0 | 1 | 2 |
| 12 | family | H | | H | | | 3 | | D | Sc | 0 | 1 | 2 |
| 13 | side | H | | | L | R | | | D | Sc | 0 | 1 | 2 |
| 14 | position | H | | | L | | 3 | | D | Sc | 0 | 1 | 2 |
| 15 | give | H | | | L | | I | | D | Sc | 0 | 1 | 2 |
| 16 | cathedral | | L | H | | | 3 | | D | Sc | 0 | 1 | 2 |
| 17 | plead | | L | | L | R | | | D | Sc | 0 | 1 | 2 |
| 18 | century | H | | | L | | 3 | | D | Sc | 0 | 1 | 2 |
| 19 | head | H | | H | | | I | | D | Sc | 0 | 1 | 2 |
| 20 | hospital | H | | H | | | 3 | | D | Sc | 0 | 1 | 2 |
| 21 | shone | | L | | L | | I | | D | Sc | 0 | 1 | 2 |
| 22 | ridicule | | L | | L | | 3 | | D | Sc | 0 | 1 | 2 |
| 23 | dread | | L | | L | | I | | D | Sc | 0 | 1 | 2 |
| 24 | blood | H | | H | | | I | | D | Sc | 0 | 1 | 2 |
| | **N** | /12 | /12 | /12 | /12 | /8 | /8 | /8 | **TOTAL SCORE** | ( | /24) | | /48 |

| Length: | 1 syllable (reg + irreg scores) | = | /16 |
|---|---|---|---|
| | 3 syllable | = | /8 |

Key: FREQ = frequency; IMAG = imageability; REG = regularity of spelling – sound; SYLL = syllables; H = high; L = low; R = regular; I = irregular

## REMAINDER OF TARGET WORDS ("INFORMATIVE" . . . "JIDDER") ARE SCORED ON THE FOLLOWING PAGES

## 21.   READING COMPLEX WORDS (P. 145 C&L)

|   | TARGET | RESPONSE | MANNER OF RESPONSE | | SCORE | | |
|---|---|---|---|---|---|---|---|
| 1 | informative | | D | Sc | 0 | 1 | 2 |
| 2 | recooked | | D | Sc | 0 | 1 | 2 |
| 3 | presenting | | D | Sc | 0 | 1 | 2 |
| | | **TOTAL SCORE** | | | | | **/6** |

## 22.   READING FUNCTION WORDS (P. 145 C&L)

|   | TARGET | RESPONSE | MANNER OF RESPONSE | | SCORE | | |
|---|---|---|---|---|---|---|---|
| 1 | but | | D | Sc | 0 | 1 | 2 |
| 2 | of | | D | Sc | 0 | 1 | 2 |
| 3 | and | | D | Sc | 0 | 1 | 2 |
| | | **TOTAL SCORE** | | | | | **/6** |

## 23.   READING NONWORDS (P. 145 C&L)

*Now these are all nonsense words. Have a go at reading those aloud.*

|   | TARGET | RESPONSE | MANNER OF RESPONSE | | SCORE | | |
|---|---|---|---|---|---|---|---|
| 1 | fask | | D | Sc | 0 | 1 | 2 |
| 2 | tib | | D | Sc | 0 | 1 | 2 |
| 3 | thirk | | D | Sc | 0 | 1 | 2 |
| 4 | deggle | | D | Sc | 0 | 1 | 2 |
| 5 | jidder | | D | Sc | 0 | 1 | 2 |
| | | **TOTAL SCORE** | | | | | **/6** |

**WRITING (SUBTESTS 24–27)**

See the C&L Test Book for instructions (pp. 146–156).

**Read instructions** from the guide in the **Test Book**.

Give this **Scoring Book** to the **person with aphasia**.

Score the results **later**. (Score sheets appear on pp. 33–34 of this book.)

_____

Please write these ALL in CAPITALS

T          C          H          A          Y

_____

(practice)
d          e          r          b          f          g

_____

cup          feet          toothbrush

_____    _____    _____

Please write the names of these pictures:

P.  _____

1.  _____

2.  _____

3.  _____

4.  _____

5.  _____

Please listen and write these words:

P. _____

1. _____

2. _____

3. _____

4. _____

5. _____


What is happening in this picture?

## 24.  WRITING: COPYING (P. 146 C&L)

|  | Letters written correctly |
|---|---|
| Copying – same case – letters | /5 |
| Copying – cross case – letters | /5 |
| Copying – cross case – words | /17 |
| **TOTAL SCORE** | **/27** |

## 25.  WRITING PICTURE NAMES (PP. 147–153 C&L)

**Disregard case.**

**Score letters not words (see Manual for example).**

(✓)   Correct letter, correct position relative to adjacent letters. Score 1

(S)   Substitution          Score 0

(O)   Omission          Score 0

(T)   Transposition          Score 0

Transposition of two adjacent letters is counted as a single error (score 0 for first letter, +1 no penalty for second letter).

(A)   Additional letters          Score – 1 from the **total** score

(regardless of how many additional letters)

(SP)  Semantically related verbal paraphasias are scored as 0

|  | TARGET | WORD TYPE | RESPONSE | TYPE OF RESPONSE (✓, S, O, T, A, SP) | LETTER SCORING (+1, 0, –1) | SCORE |
|---|---|---|---|---|---|---|
| P | hat | HiF, HiI, Reg |  |  |  |  |
| 1 | boy | HiF, HiI, Reg |  |  |  | /3 |
| 2 | eye | HiF, HiI, Irreg |  |  |  | /3 |
| 3 | pear | LoF, HiI, Reg (with homophone possibility) |  |  |  | /4 |
| 4 | tank | LoF, HiI, Reg |  |  |  | /4 |
| 5 | giraffe | LoF, HiI, Irreg |  |  |  | /7 |
|  |  |  |  |  | **TOTAL SCORE** | **/21** |

Key: F = frequency; I = imageability; Hi = high; Lo = low; Reg = regular; Irreg = irregular

## 26.  WRITING TO DICTATION (P. 154 C&L)

**Disregard case.**

| | TARGET | WORD TYPE | RESPONSE | TYPE OF RESPONSE (✓, S, O, T, A, SP) | LETTER SCORING (+1, 0, −1 see above) |
|---|---|---|---|---|---|
| P | pen | HiF, HiI, Reg | | | |
| 1 | man | HiF, HiI, Reg | | | /3 |
| 2 | yacht | LoF, HiI, Irreg | | | /5 |
| 3 | idea | LoF, LoI, Reg | | | /4 |
| 4 | undrinkable | LoF, LoI, Reg, Morph complex | | | /11 |
| 5 | blosh | nonword | | | /5 |
| | | | | **TOTAL SCORE** | **/28** |

Key: F = frequency; I = imageability; Hi = high; Lo = low; Reg = regular; Irreg = irregular; Morph complex = morphologically complex

## 27.  WRITTEN PICTURE DESCRIPTION (PP. 155–156 C&L)

| A APPROPRIATE ICWS | B INAPPROPRIATE ICWS | C GRAMMATICAL WELL-FORMEDNESS |
|---|---|---|
| | | |
| **A Total =** | **B Total =** | **C Total =** |

## TOTAL SCORE (A − B) + C =

## [[THIS IS THE END OF THE LANGUAGE SECTION]]

# PART 3: APHASIA IMPACT QUESTIONNAIRE

(Administrators should read aloud the *italicised* text and follow all other instructions.)

Read this script or, once familiar with the procedure, read the text directly from the AIQ itself.

*How are you feeling **today**?* Show 'How are you feeling' page.

If it's a negative response, check if the person wishes to carry on, delay or abandon the administration altogether.

*We're going to **talk** about **aphasia** today. Aphasia is difficulty talking, understanding, reading and writing* (point to the corresponding pictures).

*We're going to talk about **how aphasia affects life for you**. Does it affect **what you do and how you feel?***

*We're going to go through **this questionnaire**. The questions are **all** about how things have been **during the last week.***

*It is **your view** of how things are. There is **no right** or **wrong.***

*Before we start, let's **choose a scale.***

*Which person **looks** most like you?*

Person with aphasia selects appropriate image. You give the person the AIQ Rating Scale booklet showing that same image, to refer to throughout.

*I'll show you a picture and ask a question* (show Q1.). ***You will use your scale** Point to the Scale chosen by the person with aphasia.*

*I want you to think about **how things have been** in the **last week – overall** this last week.*

*Remember there is **no right or wrong answer**. It is **your** view of how things feel about **life with aphasia**, just during **this last week.***

*Let's start with a question about **you talking** to other people.*

NOW TURN TO QUESTION 1. OF THE QUESTIONNAIRE (This week ... how easy was it for you to **talk** to ...)

So, we're looking at your talking – finding words and saying a sentence.
[Reveal p. XXX of AIQ, and so on.]
*During the last week, how easy is it for you to:*

---

1. *talk to* [use person's name] ***the person closest to you****?*                                          **Rating:**  4   3   2   1   0
Present the 'This week, how easy was it to talk to [. . .] someone closest to you?' page.
NB – use the name of the person closest to them if you know it.
*if talking to X was very easy, the same as before your stroke, point here* (point to far right of the scale)
*if you couldn't talk at all, impossible, you would point here* (point to far left of the scale)
*but maybe its somewhere in between* (sweep hand across the scale).
*So, what do you think – how easy was talking with XX . . . show me on the scale?*
*So, it can be any one of these* (point to all five people on the scale)
*can you show me on the scale?* (sweep your hand across the whole scale).
*Great. That's the idea.*
**Comments**

---

2. *talk to **someone you don't know, a stranger***?                                          **Rating:**  4   3   2   1   0
Prompt if needed: suggest *". . . someone like me"*, or *". . . someone in a shop."*
**Comments**

---

*Now we are going to think about your **understanding** . . . so someone else is talking, you must follow what they say . . . So, during*
*the last week*

---

3. *how easy was it to understand* [use person's name] ***someone close to you****?*                                          **Rating:**  4   3   2   1   0
Gesture and if needed, prompt: *". . . follow what is being said."*
**Comments**

| | | | | | | |
|---|---|---|---|---|---|---|
| 4. *We are still thinking about your* **understanding** *. . . in the last week, how easy was it to understand* **someone you don't know**?<br>Prompt if needed: *"a stranger."*<br>**Comments** | **Rating:** | 4 | 3 | 2 | 1 | 0 |
| 5. *During the last week, how easy was it for you to* **write a message** *to a* **friend**?<br>Prompt: *". . . to* **find** *and* **spell** *the words", ". . . in a* **card***", ". . . in an* **email***."*<br>**Comments** | **Rating:** | 4 | 3 | 2 | 1 | 0 |
| *When you do write, do you prefer to email, text or use pen and paper?* **CIRCLE RESPONSE HERE** | | | | | | |
| 6. *During the last week, how easy was it for you to* **read** *a* **news story**?<br>Prompt: *". . . from your* **phone***", ". . . in an actual* **paper***", ". . . on a* **computer***"*<br>**Comments** | **Rating:** | 4 | 3 | 2 | 1 | 0 |

## 29. PARTICIPATION (PP. 11–14 AIQ)

*Now we are going to look at **things you had to do** this week. Prompt: "chores"*
*So overall, during the last week, if things you had to do were very easy, point here.*
*If things you had to do were very difficult, you would point here.*

**7.** *First, how easy was it for you to do things you **had to do** this week, like . . .*
**Point** to each **corresponding picture** as you identify . . .
- *Appointments?*
- *Transport?*
- *Paperwork/Money?*
- *Shopping?*
*So overall, how easy was it for you to do things you had to do this week?*
**Comments**

**Rating:** 4 3 2 1 0

**8.** *Now what about **things** you **wanted to do** this week? Were you able to do **enough positive things** you wanted to do?*
**Point** to each **corresponding picture** as you identify . . .
- *Going to groups or clubs?*
- *Holidays?*
- *Going out?*
- *Hobbies?*
*If you were able to do **lots of positive things to do**, point here.*
*If you **couldn't do any** positive things, you point here.*
**Comments**

**Rating:** 4 3 2 1 0

**9.** *Now we are going to think about your **friends**.*
*So, during the last week, **how** were **things** with your **friends**?*
*If things with your **friends were very good** this week, point here.*
*If things with your friends were very difficult, point here.*
**Comments**

**Rating:** 4 3 2 1 0

**10.** *Now we are going to think about your **family**.*
*(There are three diverse family groups. Use whichever group the person chooses.)*
*So, during the last week, how were things with your family?*
*If **things** with your **family** were **very good** this week, point here.*
*If things with your family were **very difficult**, point here.*
**Comments**

**Rating:** 4 3 2 1 0

## 30.　EMOTIONAL WELLBEING (PP. 15–25 AIQ)

*Now there are some questions about **how you've felt** this week. We have talked to **other people with aphasia**. They **told us** how they feel sometimes.*

*Can we **check** if **you share these feelings** or not? Let's start with **frustration**.*

Monitor the person's reactions closely. If they are struggling, ascertain if they wish to carry on.

| | |
|---|---|
| 11. *So, this week, have you **felt frustrated**?*<br>*If you have felt very frustrated, you would point here.*<br>*If you have not felt at all frustrated, point here.*<br>*Or it could be somewhere in between.*<br>Prompt: " . . . wound up"<br>**Comments** | **Rating:**　4　3　2　1　0 |
| 12. *What about being worried, have you felt **worried** this week?*<br>Prompt: " . . . anxious"<br>**Comments** | **Rating:**　4　3　2　1　0 |
| 13. *During the last week, have you felt **unhappy**?*<br>Prompt: " . . . sad"<br>**Comments** | **Rating:**　4　3　2　1　0 |
| 14. *Some people have told us they feel helpless. Have you felt **helpless** this week?*<br>Prompt: " . . . powerless"<br>**Comments** | **Rating:**　4　3　2　1　0 |
| 15. *Have you felt **bored**?*<br>Prompt: " . . . nothing interesting"<br>**Comments** | **Rating:**　4　3　2　1　0 |

16. *During the last week, have you felt **embarrassed**?*
Prompt: *" . . . ashamed"*
**Comments**

**Rating:** 4 3 2 1 0

17. *Have you felt **angry** this week?*
Prompt: *" . . . cross"*
**Comments**

**Rating:** 4 3 2 1 0

18. *During the last week, have you felt **isolated**?*
Prompt: *" . . . on your own/cut off"*
**Comments**

**Rating:** 4 3 2 1 0

19. *I **know** that you are **not stupid**, but **some people** tell us they **sometimes feel stupid**.*
*During the **last week**, have you felt **stupid**?*
Prompt: *" . . . feeling daft"*
Note: Administrators can often feel uncomfortable asking this question, but it has been extensively researched with people with aphasia and they do not share the same misgivings. When specifically asked about this question, no-one has felt it should be removed. Instead, they report it was an important opportunity to discuss whether they do or don't *feel stupid*.
**Comments**

**Rating:** 4 3 2 1 0

20. *Do you feel **confident**?*
Prompt: *" . . . assured"*
**Comments**

**Rating:** 4 3 2 1 0

21. *Now we are thinking about the **future** .*
*During the last week, how have you felt about the future?*
Prompt: *" . . . optimistic?"*
**Comments**

**Rating:** 4 3 2 1 0

**'Enjoy?' page P. 26**
*Are there things you **enjoy** doing these days?* **DO NOT RATE**
Prompt: "... like to do?"

| | | |
|---|---|---|
| Going for a drive | Being with family | Enjoying music |
| Gardening | Doing something creative e.g., drawing | Seeing a friend |
| Seeing lots of friends | Caring for a pet | A social club e.g., bowling, bingo, wine club |
| Going outside e.g., going for a walk | Something physical e.g., going for a swim | Being pampered e.g., having a haircut |

**'Anything else?' page**
*Is there **anything else** you'd like to add about life with aphasia for you?*

Thank the person for completing the assessment.

If it feels appropriate, give a condensed summary of what the person has expressed, and if negative emotions have been expressed, confirm that now can be the hardest time, that you are there to help and that sharing their experiences and feeling will help plan therapy that works for them.

Ensure enough time for more relaxed conversation before finishing.

# [[THIS IS THE END OF THE APHASIA IMPACT QUESTIONNAIRE]]

# MASTER SCORE SHEET

| Subtest/Section | TEST 1 | | | TEST 2 | | | TEST 3 | | | Cut-off Score |
|---|---|---|---|---|---|---|---|---|---|---|
| **COGNITIVE SCREEN** | Number Correct | Score | T-Score* | Number Correct | Score | T-Score* | Number Correct | Score | T-Score* | |
| 1. Line bisection | | | | | | | | | | ±2.5 |
| 2. Semantic memory<br>Error types:**<br>Close semantic — TEST 1 /10, TEST 2 /10, TEST 3 /10<br>Distant semantic — TEST 1 /10, TEST 2 /10, TEST 3 /10<br>Unrelated — TEST 1 /10, TEST 2 /10, TEST 3 /10 | | /10 | | | /10 | | | /10 | | 8/10 |
| 3. Word fluency  TEST 1  TEST 2  TEST 3<br>Animals:<br>"s":<br>Total: | | | | | | | | | | 13 |
| 4. Recognition memory | | /10 | | | /10 | | | /10 | | 8/10 |
| 5. Gesture object use | | /12 | | | /12 | | | /12 | | 9/10 |
| 6. Arithmetic | | /6 | | | /6 | | | /6 | | 1/6 |
| **Cognitive TOTAL** | | /38 | | | /38 | | | /38 | | |

**LANGUAGE BATTERY**

## Part 1: Language comprehension (note order of subtests)

| Subtest/Section | TEST 1 | | | TEST 2 | | | TEST 3 | | | Cut-off Score |
|---|---|---|---|---|---|---|---|---|---|---|
| | Number Correct | Score | T-Score* | Number Correct | Score | T-Score* | Number Correct | Score | T-Score* | |
| *Comprehension of spoken language* | | | | | | | | | | |
| 7. Comprehension of spoken words<br>Error types:**   TEST 1   TEST 2   TEST 3<br>Phonological  /15  /15  /15<br>Semantic    /15  /15  /15<br>Unrelated   /15  /15  /15 | /15 | /30 | | /15 | /30 | | /15 | /30 | | 25/30 |
| 9. Comprehension of spoken sentences | /16 | /32 | | /16 | /32 | | /16 | /32 | | 27/32 |
| 11. Comprehension of spoken paragraphs | | /4 | | | /4 | | | /4 | | 2/4 |
| **Comprehension of spoken language TOTAL** | | **/66** | | | **/66** | | | **/66** | | **56/66** |
| *Comprehension of written language* | | | | | | | | | | |
| 8. Comprehension of written words<br>Error types:**   TEST 1   TEST 2   TEST 3<br>Phonological  /15  /15  /15<br>Semantic    /15  /15  /15<br>Unrelated   /15  /15  /15 | /15 | /30 | | /15 | /30 | | /15 | /30 | | 27/30 |
| 10. Comprehension of written sentences | /16 | /32 | | /16 | /32 | | /16 | /32 | | 23/32 |
| **Comprehension of written language TOTAL** | | **/62** | | | **/62** | | | **/62** | | **53/66** |

Continued…

| Subtest/Section | TEST 1 | | | TEST 2 | | | TEST 3 | | | Cut-off Score |
|---|---|---|---|---|---|---|---|---|---|---|
| | Number Correct | Score | T-Score* | Number Correct | Score | T-Score* | Number Correct | Score | T-Score* | |
| **Part 2: Expressive language** | | | | | | | | | | |
| *Repetition* | | | | | | | | | | |
| 12. Repetition of words | /16 | /32 | | /16 | /32 | | /16 | /32 | | 29/32 |
| 13. Repetition of complex words | /3 | /6 | | /3 | /6 | | /3 | /6 | | 5/6 |
| 14. Repetition of nonwords | /5 | /10 | | /5 | /10 | | /5 | /10 | | 5/10 |
| 15. Repetition of digit strings | /14 | /14 | | /14 | /14 | | /14 | /14 | | 8/10 (span of 4) |
| 16. Repetition of sentences | /12 | /12 | | /12 | /12 | | /12 | /12 | | 10/12 (span of 5) |
| **Repetition TOTAL** | **/50** | **/74** | | **/50** | **/74** | | **/50** | **/74** | | **67/74** |
| *Spoken language production* | | | | | | | | | | |
| 17. Naming objects | /24 | /48 | | /24 | /48 | | /24 | /48 | | 43/48 |
| Use of phonological cues | | | | | | | | | | |
| 18. Naming actions | /5 | /10 | | /5 | /10 | | /5 | /10 | | 8/10 |
| Word fluency TOTAL (subtest 3 from COGNITIVE SCREEN) | | | | | | | | | | |
| **Naming TOTAL (sum objects/actions/fluency)** | | | | | | | | | | **69** |
| *Spoken picture description* | | | | | | | | | | |
| 19. Spoken picture description | | | | | | | | | | 33 |
| *Reading aloud* | | | | | | | | | | |
| 20. Reading words | /24 | /48 | | /24 | /48 | | /24 | /48 | | 45/48 |
| 21. Reading complex words | /3 | /6 | | /3 | /6 | | /3 | /6 | | 4/6 |
| 22. Reading function words | /3 | /6 | | /3 | /6 | | /3 | /6 | | 3/6 |
| 23. Reading nonwords | /5 | /10 | | /5 | /10 | | /5 | /10 | | 6/10 |
| **Reading TOTAL** | **/35** | **/70** | | **/35** | **/70** | | **/35** | **/70** | | **58/70** |

| Subtest/Section | TEST 1 | | | TEST 2 | | | TEST 3 | | | Cut-off Score |
|---|---|---|---|---|---|---|---|---|---|---|
| | Number Correct | Score | T-Score* | Number Correct | Score | T-Score* | Number Correct | Score | T-Score* | |
| *Writing* | | | | | | | | | | |
| 24. Writing: Copying | | /27 | | | /27 | | | /27 | | 25/27 |
| 25. Writing picture names | | /21 | | | /21 | | | /21 | | 15/21 |
| 26. Writing to dictation | | /28 | | | /28 | | | /28 | | 24/28 |
| **Writing TOTAL** | | **/76** | | | **/76** | | | **/76** | | **66/76** |
| *Written picture description* | | | | | | | | | | |
| 27. Written picture description | | | | | | | | | | 19 |

| Part 3: Aphasia Impact Questionnaire - Concise |
|---|

| | Number Correct | Score | T-Score* | Number Correct | Score | T-Score* | Number Correct | Score | T-Score* | Cut-off Score |
|---|---|---|---|---|---|---|---|---|---|---|
| 28. Communication | | /24 | | | /24 | | | /24 | | *** |
| 29. Participation | | /16 | | | /16 | | | /16 | | *** |
| 30. Emotional well-being | | /44 | | | /44 | | | /44 | | *** |
| **AIQ TOTAL** | | **/84** | | | **/84** | | | **/84** | | *** |

Cognitive Screen subtests score 0/1, except "Gesture object use" (0/1/2).
Language Battery subtests score 0/1/2 (see p. 12 of this book for scoring instructions).
*    Calculate T-scores from tables in Appendices 2–7.
* *   Error types are given for reference only and do not affect scores.
* * *  There are no cut-off scores for AIQ items, as the questionnaire was not attempted with people with non-aphasic language.

# T-SCORE PROFILE TEMPLATE

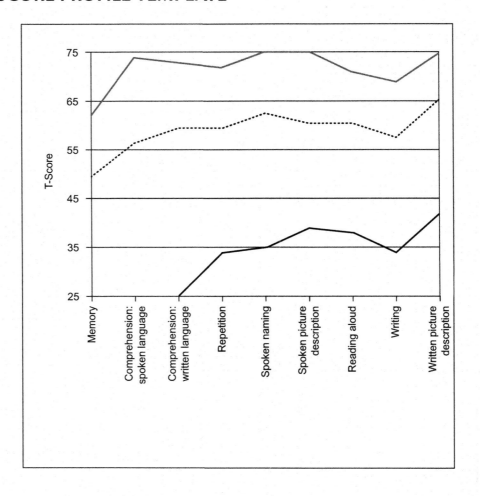